BOY'S GUIDE to GIRLS

Also by Big Book Press

Boy's Body Guide

Book of Bad Habits

Boy's Fitness Guide

Girl's Fitness Guide

BOY'S GUIDE TO GIRLS

Gary J. Campbell
Frank C. Hawkins

BOY'S GUIDE BOOKS

Published in the United States by Boy's Guide Books,
an imprint of Big Book Press. All rights reserved.

Copyright © 2012 by Big Book Press, LLC

Boy's guide to girls/by Gary J. Campbell and Frank
C. Hawkins 1. Juvenile Nonfiction/Boys & Men. 2.
Juvenile Nonfiction/Social Issues/Dating & Sex.
3. Juvenile Nonfiction/Social Issues/Emotions &
Feelings. 4. Teens.

Second printing, 2015

Library of Congress Control No: 2011961121

ISBN: 978-0-9793219-5-5

www.boysguidebooks.com

Contents

Hi Guys,

Girls have always been part of your life. But until lately, you and your friends did your thing and the girls did theirs. Now guys are talking about how to kiss a girl and who they're asking to the school dance. Girls and guys are texting and instant messaging each other. Everyone sits together at lunch, and some even walk home together in pairs after school.

How you feel about girls is changing. You have a million questions. What's the best way to tell a girl that you like her? What does it mean when she teases you? Should you go to the school dance even though you can't dance? Why bother with girls at all when there are so many other things to do?

This book will help guide you and answer your questions. It will help you understand the changes you're going through, and it will give you pointers on how to handle yourself around girls now that they're becoming a bigger part of your life. Most of all, this book will help you stay true to yourself and be ready when the girl of your dreams comes along.

Sincerely,

Gary "Soup" Campbell

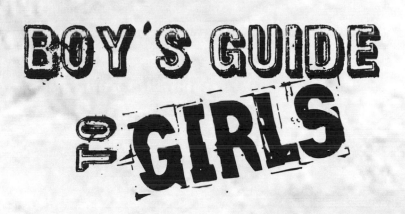

*First love is only a little foolishness
and a lot of curiosity.*

**George Bernard Shaw
(1856–1950)**

What's Going On?

One minute all you can think about is football. The next all you can think about is girls. It's just one of the many changes you'll experience during puberty. That's the time when you become an adult. Get ready because your body and the way you think about everything is going to change. Your pituitary gland starts the ball rolling, hormones flow and things will never be the same.

Hormones make you tick. Think of them as chemical messengers that are produced by your body to stimulate your tissues and cells into action. You'll see some of the changes these hormones cause, such as when hair sprouts under your arms and on your chin. You'll hear some of the changes, such as when your voice gets deeper. And there are other changes you won't see or hear, such as the new feelings you have for the pretty girl in science class.

Most boys begin puberty when they're about 12 years old. Girls, though, generally start the process two years earlier. This means that while you're in middle school, most girls your age will be more physically and emotionally mature—at least until everyone gets to high school. It also means that a lot of girls are interested in boys before boys their age are interested in them. That simple little difference in timing can cause lots of confusion and hurt feelings—for both girls and boys.

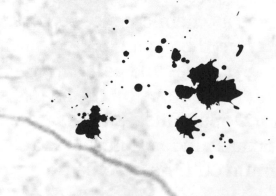

Crushes

You can't stop thinking about her. You feel great. You're excited and happy. You're on top of the world. Don't look now, but you have a crush!

Crushes are part of growing up. Just as your body changes as you get older, your emotions and feelings change, too.

Crushes are a kind of early romantic feeling. They are strong, short-lived emotions toward a girl or woman you may or may not know.

She could be your sister's friend or an older girl in the neighborhood. Maybe it's the girl your brother is dating. She could even be your teacher or someone you've seen in the movies or on TV.

No matter who it is, chances are good that you don't know your crush well, if at all. And getting to know her romantically may not be practical, but that doesn't stop you from idealizing and dreaming about her. Then, just as fast as your crush started, it ends.

Now you have a new crush. It's different this time, though. She's in your homeroom and best of all, she likes you, too. This is when things start to get interesting.

How do you know you have a crush? If three or more of these describe how you act, chances are good that you do.

1. You write her name and yours side-by-side, over and over.

2. She's all you think about.

3. She's all you talk about.

4. You don't know exactly why you like her, you just do.

5. Thinking about her makes you smile.

Liking a Girl

Having good friends is important. Hanging out, competing in sports, and playing video games with the guys is part of growing up. But what about girls?

Well, chances are good you have friends that just happen to be girls. You like hanging out with them, too, because they're easy to talk with and they like the same things you do.

You're just friends, right? There could come a time, though, when you find your feelings for a female friend beginning to change. Hmmm, is she a friend or something more—a "girlfriend"? All of a sudden, you may not be so sure.

What is it about a particular girl that makes you like her? Does she tell funny jokes, have a nice smile, flirt with you or kick a mean soccer ball? Is she pretty, outgoing or quiet? Does she wear glasses or have long blond hair? The combinations are almost endless. Fact is, certain combinations appeal to you more than others.

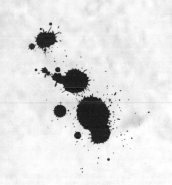

Getting to Know a Girl

One day soon you may find yourself looking at a girl and thinking, "How can I get to know her better?" For starters, be friendly, smile and say hi. There's nothing like a smile to break the ice.

If you have a friend who knows her, get them to introduce you. This is a great icebreaker. Plus, they can say some nice things about you.

If you don't have any common friends, take a chance and introduce yourself. If she's in your math class, for example, offer her the use of your calculator or ask to borrow a piece of paper or pencil. After she responds, say, "By the way, my name's Garrett. What's yours?" It may sound cheesy, but it breaks the ice and lets her know you're interested.

Now that you've been introduced, keep the ball rolling. Smile and say hi when you see her in the hallway. Engage her in conversation. You could comment about the science assignment or the math test.

Don't try too hard or say too much. The "small talk"—as it's called—gets things started to see if there's something there. Just stay relaxed and let the conversation happen.

Here are some ideas to get a conversation started:

Did you see Lady Gaga's new music video? How do you think they got her costume to light up like that?

(It can be fun to talk about something you've both experienced, like a show or video.)

How did your volleyball team do last night?

(Ask about her activities. It shows you're interested in what she's doing.)

HOW did you do on that math homework?

(This shows your willingness to help out.)

Can you believe I showed up at 4 o'clock this morning to watch for meteors with my science class? On a cloudy morning!

(Making light of yourself shows you're relaxed and approachable and don't take things too seriously.)

A great way to get to know someone is to find things you have in common. Does she shoot pool, play chess, ice skate, hang out at the mall or play an instrument? The activities you both like are a great way to get to know each other. It's a whole lot easier to feel relaxed with a person if you're both having fun shooting baskets, playing video games or riding your bikes—not just sitting across from each other trying to think of what to say next.

THE SCOOP FROM SOUP:

Be her friend first. That's the best way to find out whether you like each other as friends or if something more is possible.

Getting to know a girl takes time. Don't come on too strong and talk about dating right away or you'll probably scare her off—not to mention she might think you're a little creepy.

Go for it. The very least that will happen is you'll likely make a new friend and meet some new people.

What Is She Thinking?

There's a girl you really like. You want her to know how you feel. Yet you're not sure how, or even if, you should tell her. What if she doesn't feel the same way about you? You don't want to be embarrassed or hurt. What if you say the wrong thing?

Telling a girl you like her can be scary. Some guys never say a word because they can't get past their fear of being rejected. You can cut your chances of being embarrassed or hurt, though, by taking some time to understand the signals girls send.

Every girl says, "I like you," in a different way.

Teasing is how I let a boy know I like him. —Abby

Just like boys, some girls show friendship by teasing and picking on each other in a good-natured way. They do the same with boys they like. If a girl gives you a funny nickname, for example, it can be a pretty good sign she likes you—maybe more than just as a friend.

Boys like it when you flirt. I do it for fun. —Gabriela

Girls and boys flirt with each other all the time. Usually, it's a way to show that you're interested in the other person. Sometimes, though, people flirt to amuse themselves. So be careful when a girl flirts with you. It's usually a good sign; just remember it may not be what you think.

I'm kind of shy so I don't talk to boys much. —Olivia

Shy girls speak with their eyes. They'll look down and away, look up at you, and then look down and back again. It's a way of introducing themselves and showing you they want to talk. Try starting out by just saying hi. Be soft spoken and low key when talking with a girl who is shy.

I can't stop giggling when I'm around a guy I really like. —Emma

Does she laugh a lot when you talk to her, even though you aren't trying to be funny? Does she act a little nervous? Do her cheeks blush? Do her words get mixed up when she talks? Does she play with her hair or fidget when you're around? Those are all very good signs she's interested.

Well, when I like a guy, I kind of try to show off around him. — Rachael

"Hey, look at me!" That's the message girls are sending if they do or say things to get your attention. It's generally a good sign if a girl talks loudly around you, acts up, tries to be funny, or does things to impress you.

If I like a guy, I try to be near him and touch his arm while we're talking. It shows him I'm interested.
—Camila

Some girls, like Camila, show interest through physical gestures, such as light touches on your arm or shoulder. Keep in mind, though, it's not true for everyone. There are people—male and female—who touch people while they talk with them. It just means, "I'm listening."

Are there more signals to be on the lookout for? You bet. Here are just a few:

1. Her friends laugh and whisper in her ear when you walk by.

2. She listens to your every word.

3. She smiles at you non-stop.

4. She touches your arm or hugs you to say hello and goodbye.

5. She looks at you a lot.

6. She always tries to be your lab partner.

7. She always searches for you, whether at the football game or a school dance.

8. She asks your friends questions about you.

THE SCOOP FROM SOUP:

Speak up. How will she know you like her if you don't tell her?

What Girls Want

There's a girl in homeroom who's
tall, smart and sassy. She has freckles
and red hair. There's another girl
in language arts who's about your
height. She's pretty, sweet, has
long brown hair and always dresses
nicely. Then, there's the girl in gym
class. She's shorter than you, moody,
mischievous, with black hair and a
very pretty face. You like the girl in
homeroom best. There's something
about her red hair and tomboy
attitude that makes you feel good.

Like you, girls size up boys and
rate them according to how they
look, dress and act. Depending on
how girls see you, they might think
you're smart, cute, geeky or a jock.
If you wear Left-4-Dead t-shirts and

talk about making YouTube videos showing Modern Warfare glitches, most girls will label you as a gamer. They won't know—because they don't see—the other side of you that you keep hidden: a sensitive guy who writes songs and plays guitar.

It's a fact that people see you differently than you see yourself. "If she would just give me a chance," you say to yourself. Well, unless she sees in you a quality she likes or something the two of you have in common, she probably won't give you a second look.

And that's okay. Don't try to be someone you're not. Remember, for every girl who likes jocks, there's another girl who likes sensitive, guitar-playing gamers.

Here are some of the more popular labels girls have for guys. Do you see yourself?

JOCK: Athletic, good body, dresses well, socially popular. The guy everyone knows.

HOT: Great body, handsome face, stylish hair, always dresses well. May seem out of a girl's league, making some girls want them all the more.

FUNNY: Always smiling, tells lots of jokes, good sense of humor, fun to be around, often likes to be the center of attention. May have a hard time being serious.

NICE: Solid, all-around guy, average body, dresses okay, polite, friendly, easy-going personality. Nice guys may have to try a little harder because they don't stand out in a crowd. The guy girls are "friends" with.

GAMER: Quiet, shy, geeky, disengaged, messy hair, grungy.

May look like they're day dreaming all the time.

SMART: Studious, eccentric, a little nerdy, hair and clothes usually out of style. May have a hard time fitting in socially.

BAD Boy: Rebellious, looking to be noticed, makes it a point not to fit in, "tough guy" attitude, sometimes rowdy and loud. May be a bully.

ROCKER: Cool demeanor, funky clothes, dyed hair, body piercings, usually thin. Always talking about rock, punk or metal. Super "hot" for girls into their kind of music.

PLAYER: Good-looking, ingratiating, smooth, overly charming, makes it a point to be noticed. Considers himself a ladies' man. Has a reputation for "using" girls.

THE SCOOP FROM SOUP:

Be youself. There's no need to be anyone other than who you are. After all, the "real" you is the person who caught her eye in the first place.

How to Say, "I Like You!"

You've been watching the signs and you're pretty sure the girl in homeroom likes you. There's no doubt in your mind that you like her. Every day that goes by, every time you see her, you want to say, "I like you, let's do something together." But, how do you do that?

Some guys write notes, others have their friends do the talking and some just blurt it out. Writing down on paper the way you feel is okay, but you can never be sure who, besides her, might read it. Having friends tell her how you feel is okay, but who better than you can say what's on your mind? Blurting out your feelings is okay, too, but it would probably go over better if you thought things out and had something more to say than, "Hey! I like you!"

Here are a few tried-and-true ways to tell her how you feel:

1. Sit across from her on the bus and strike up a conversation. If you both have a good time, do it again tomorrow.

2. Tell her you thought her science project was really great. Ask if she wants to be your lab partner next time.

3. Ask her to dance at the school dance.

4. Ask her and her friends to join you and your friends in a game of kickball.

5. Offer her the extra ticket you have to the class play.

6. Go see her step team perform and ask if she'd like to come to your lacrosse game.

7. Call her on the phone and ask her about the science homework. Take the opportunity to chat a little about school and her friends.

8. Invite her and her friends to a movie with you and your friends.

9. Ask if she wants to volunteer with you and some friends for the Earth Day community cleanup.

10. Let her know that you and your friends will be at McDonald's after school. Suggest she bring her friends and meet you all there.

Did you notice that the words, "I like you," aren't anywhere to be seen? That's because you don't need to say it. The fact that you like a girl is obvious because you're being so friendly. And if she's interested in you, she'll accept your invitations.

If she's not interested, all she has to say is, "No thanks, I don't feel like dancing." That's a lot easier for her to say and for you to hear than, "No, I don't like you."

Daily Don'ts

Okay, now she knows you're interested. She and her friends came by Mickey D's on Tuesday after school to say hi. Since then, though, the two of you haven't gotten together. You've asked, but it just doesn't happen for one reason or another.

This is when you want to play it smart and avoid the everyday mistakes guys make when things aren't going just right.

MONDAY: Don't be too pushy. Most girls don't like it. Back off and give her some space.

TUESDAY: Don't try to *make* her like you. You're in charge of your feelings, but you're not in charge of hers.

WEDNESDAY: Don't bad-mouth other guys to make youself look good. In the end, it just makes you look bad.

THURSDAY: Don't show off to impress her. It will draw attention to you, but not the kind you want.

FRIDAY: Don't try to make her feel sorry for you. Girls don't want a guy who looks desperate and emotionally weak.

What If She Says No?

Okay, so this wasn't what you were expecting. You were sure she liked you more than just as a friend. Her girlfriend told you she did. She flirted with you, teased you, and you hung out in the same group. You played it low key and took your time to be sure about how she felt.

This morning you were on top of the world. Now you feel sick to your stomach. It hurts. You feel alone. This is exactly the situation you wanted to avoid. What you need to do now is:

- Smile and say, "That's okay. I hope we can still be friends."

- Stay busy with other things, such as schoolwork or sports.

- Hang out with your friends. It will take your mind off your feelings.

- Stay cool and make a joke about it. Laughing will make you feel better and show everyone you're doing just fine.

- Remember that she's not the only girl in the world. Why would you want to be with someone who doesn't want to be with you?

- Talk to someone you trust, such as a friend, family member, teacher or school counselor. They can help you make sense of your feelings and move on.

And here's what you *don't* need to do:

- Don't try to change her mind.

- Don't get mad, try to get even, trash talk her to your friends, or send nasty emails or text messages.

- Don't ask a friend (or one of her friends) to get involved on your behalf.

- Don't have a pity-party to feel sorry for yourself. It will only make you feel worse.

- Don't ask her next week if she's changed her mind.

- Don't keep thinking about her and what could have been.

THE SCOOP FROM SOUP:

When you really like a girl, it's hard to take no for an answer. Just because she's nice, friendly, and fun to be around, it doesn't mean she wants to be your girlfriend. If you force yourself on her, she'll start avoiding you. If you want to be friends at all, back off and take it easy.

Unattainable Girls

Maybe she just won best Movie Actress at the Teen Choice Awards. Maybe she's a swimsuit model. She could be that senior girl on the volleyball team or the new 8th grade teacher all the guys are talking about. Whoever it is, if you have feelings for a girl that aren't—or can't be—returned, it can be a tough pill to swallow once you realize what's happening. So just how do you get girls like that out of your system?

STAY BUSY. Call your friends. Try something new. Join a group. Start a new project. Volunteer for something. Make new friends. Do anything except sit or mope around feeling sorry for yourself.

CLEAN HOUSE. You know all that stuff—the pictures, posters, movie ticket stubs—you have laying around the house and hanging on the wall? They're meant to remind you of her, and guess what, that's exactly what they do. Do yourself a favor. Sit down in the quiet, look at everything one last time and then chuck it all in the trashcan.

TAKE A BREAK. Let some time pass. As you can, avoid going to places and activities that put you in contact with her or remind you of her. It won't be long before you're feeling better and things are back to normal.

START AGAIN. Get to know other girls who are close to your age, go to your school or live in your neighborhood. Be realistic—no movie stars this time around. You may think you'll never feel the same about anyone again. Not true. In time, you'll meet a great girl who you really like. And this time, she'll like you back.

How to Say No to a Girl

There's this girl who sits next to you in band. You can tell she likes you in a girlfriend-boyfriend way. But you don't feel the same about her. The all-school spring dance is coming up and you know she's going to ask you. You're nervous. You don't know how to say no without hurting her feelings. It's the same feeling you got when another girl asked you to the movies last year. Why does all this boy-girl stuff have to be so difficult?

Saying no is hard to do. But you need to say it if that's how you feel. If she asks you to the dance, you don't want to lead her on by saying yes. That wouldn't be fair to either you or her. Especially when there's someone else you really want to go with.

Here are a few pointers to make turning down the offer of a date a little easier. Remember, it's not only what you say, but how you say it.

BE HONEST AND TO THE POINT. Saying, "No thanks. I'm flattered you asked me, but I don't want to," is better than, "Well, uh, I don't know. Maybe, but I don't think so right now. Sorry." Don't leave her confused by sending mixed signals. And don't say, "We can still be friends" if you don't mean it.

BE POLITE. Everyone deserves to be treated with respect. It takes a lot of guts to tell someone how you feel. Give her your attention, look her in the eyes, and use polite words: "It's very nice of you to ask me, but I have other plans for the dance."

BE FIRM. If she doesn't take no for an answer, keeps hanging around, and you don't want the attention, use stronger language to get your point across. Try something like this: "I don't want to hurt your feelings, but I'm not interested. I have to go now, and I would like you to leave me alone."

BE DISCREET. Don't make it a big deal that she asked you out and you said "no way." There's no need to talk about it with anyone. You wouldn't want the fact that someone turned you down spread all over school, would you? Remember, next time you might be on the receiving end.

THE SCOOP FROM SOUP:

Let's say a girl asks you out and you think she's ugly, unpopular, or dresses weird and acts even weirder. You don't want to be seen with her, let alone be her boyfriend. You can't imagine why she would think you're interested in her. Well, forget all that and remember the guts it takes to ask someone out. She has feelings just like you do. Just say, "no thanks," and move on. Don't make her the butt of jokes with your friends to prop up your own self-esteem. Making fun of people—for any reason—is one of the meanest and most hurtful things you can do.

Are You Ready?

You may be wondering if now's the right time to get serious about girls. Maybe you're not sure if you're ready. Your best friend already has a "steady" girlfriend. You might be asking yourself, "Should I have one, too?"

Here are five questions that will help you figure it out. Take a look and see if they sound like you. Circle your answer to each question.

1. Your best friend talks about nothing but girls. You'd rather go bike riding and play video games like "us" guys used to.

   Yes or No

2. The cousin of your best friend's girlfriend is visiting this summer. He wants to "set you up" with her. You feel queasy and not sure how to handle it.

Yes Or No

3. You're interested in a girl or two at school. But when you think about the gossip, teasing, and getting dumped, you feel it's just not worth the trouble.

Yes Or No

4. One of the girls in your class hangs around you all the time. She told your best friend she'd go out with you if you asked her. It makes you feel really uncomfortable. You just don't want to deal with the situation.

Yes Or No

5. Your parents drop you at the movie theater to meet your best friend. To your surprise,

his girlfriend and her cousin are with him. You're upset and want to get out of there.

Yes **Or** No

THE ANSWERS:

You Are Ready

Every no answer is an indication you're ready for a new kind of relationship with girls. The more no answers you have, the more ready you are.

You Are Not Ready

If you answered mostly yes, you're probably not ready. That's okay. Everyone is on their own schedule when it comes to girls. Just as some young men get hair on their faces first, others get interested in girls first. Don't rush it. There is plenty of time and plenty of girls to go around. You'll know when the time is right.

Girl Crazy. Who, Me?

Are you girl crazy? How would you know if you were? What difference does it make? Let's take a look and see. Circle a, b or c below.

1. You're ice skating with friends when a girl you know walks into the snack bar looking really great, with her hair pulled back and her skates draped over her shoulder.

   a. You catch her eye, smile, and keep talking with your friends.

   b. You watch her walk by and disappear around the corner. You lose track of what you're talking about with your friends.

c. Friends? What friends? You take off and follow her.

2. You're camping with a youth group for the weekend. Half the group is going water skiing and the other half is hiking. You love hiking and have been looking forward to it for weeks. A girl you really like says she's going water skiing.

   a. You tell her you'll see her when you get back. You lace up your boots, double check your daypack, and head over to the trailhead.

   b. You try to talk her into going on the hike. So what if she doesn't have the right boots or a pack? You can loan her yours, right?

   c. You decide to blow off the hike (and your friends) and head back to camp for your swimsuit.

3. District ensemble competition is this weekend, it's already Thursday and you need to practice your trumpet.

    a. You get out the music, sit down, and practice.

    b. You get out the music, sit down, and mostly daydream about a girl who gave you her number last weekend when you were at the mall with your friends.

    c. You try calling the number. She doesn't answer—any of the four times you try. Fifteen minutes later you take off to the mall in hopes of running into her.

4. During lunch, a very pretty girl comes in with her friends and they sit at the table across from you.

    a. You notice her and keep talking with your friends.

   b. You try not to stare at her, but you can't help yourself.

   c. You start to talk louder and show off so she'll notice you.

5. You make a list of all the girls you've kissed—or tried to kiss.

   a. Okay, maybe one.

   b. You can count them on one hand.

   c. You feel like hot stuff because you can't remember them all.

THE ANSWERS:

MOSTLY *a's*

You're self-sufficient. You like yourself. You're confident and have self-respect. You don't need a girlfriend to be complete. Sure, it would be great to have a girlfriend, but you're just fine without one, too. You are your own man, as they say.

Mostly *b*'s

You're positive and hopeful about meeting a girl who likes you just as you are. You're willing to meet girls halfway when it comes to getting together, but your life doesn't revolve around them. You have other priorities in your life, too, like sports, school, friends, and your quest to find the best cheese dog in town.

Mostly *c*'s

Girls are your #1 priority. To be honest, you sound a little carried away, maybe even girl crazy. Maybe you're the guy who'll do anything to find a steady girlfriend so you don't feel left out of the dating scene. Maybe you're the guy who wants to go out with a new girl every week because it makes you feel like a big shot in front of other guys. Neither one is the right reason to get together. Consider taking it easy on the girls for a while. Pay more attention to yourself. If you think you're worth it, so will they.

Tell Me the Rules

Wait—there are rules?

Well, yes and no. Nothing is written in stone and there's no Code of Conduct posted for all to see. However, society does have common-sense guidelines—unwritten rules—that tell us what is and what isn't okay when it comes to dating and girls.

You already know some of the rules. But just in case you missed any, here a few to consider.

Q: *I'm 17 and she's 13. Is it okay to date a younger girl?*

A: Lots of girls get crushes on older boys. Your younger sister's best friend or the girl next door are good examples of younger girls who might all of a sudden take a liking to you. There's lots of flirting and general talk about "getting together." It's a lot of fun, and hopefully you both know it's a game. And while that's fine, it begins and ends right there.

So, is it okay to have a romantic relationship with a 13-year-old girl if you're in high school? No, it's not. You and a 13-year-old girl are at entirely different stages of growing up. Sure, it's tempting because she doesn't know the rules and you have the advantage.

Even if you think she's cute and she really likes you, in the end, it's not fair to either you or her. If you're sure it's meant to happen, wait until she's in high school and see if those two years make a difference in how either of you think.

THE SCOOP FROM SOUP:

The older you get, the less the age difference matters. Eight years doesn't seem so much when you're 35 and she's 27. But that same eight-year difference is much bigger when you're 18 and she's 10. If you like to date younger girls, wait until you're older and the age difference is no longer as important.

Q: *At what age is it okay to have a girlfriend?*

A: This decision is between you and your parents. The answer will depend on their beliefs, your age, and what you mean by "girlfriend." Lots of guys in middle school ask girls out on dates. There's lots of talk about going to dinner and the other things they see their parents do. But not much really happens in the way of actually going anywhere outside of school and school-related activities.

It's more likely your first "relationship" with a girl will consist of texting, talking on the phone, and hanging out at school in a group of friends. As you get a little older, you and your friends will probably go to school dances or movies with a bunch of girls, knowing that some of you are sort of paired off. Then as you get even older, you and a girl may decide to go out on an actual date.

Q: *How many times should I ask a girl out if she says no?*

A: Every situation is different and it takes experience to judge when enough is enough. As a general rule, though, if she responds with, "I'd like to, but I can't make it this time," give her the benefit of the doubt and ask her again later. If she says the same thing a second time, it's probably her way of saying no.

If she gives you a clear no or a good reason, like "I have a boyfriend" or

"My parents won't let me date until I'm 16," then one time is enough. It's tempting to go back later and ask, "Are you sure you won't change your mind?" but, the best thing to do is gracefully accept the no and move on.

Q: *Is it okay to go out with your best friend's girlfriend?*

A: Yes, *if* you're going out as friends and all three of you know what's going on.

Absolutely not if you and his girlfriend have romantic feelings for each other and you're doing it behind your friend's back. Situations like this happen, but before you two act on your feelings, understand that it could ruin the friendship between you and your best friend. Most of all, don't do anything without everyone being open and honest about what's happening. That means she needs to end her relationship with your best friend *before* you go out with her.

THE SCOOP FROM SOUP:

If you do decide to go out with your best friend's ex-girlfriend, it's a good idea to let the dust settle after they break up. In other words, give it some time. When things do calm down, you might even try checking with your friend to let him know your intentions. This can be a mighty uncomfortable thing to do, but it could save your friendship.

Dances and Parties

You've been invited to your first girl-guy party. Everyone is talking, and you have lots of questions.

Q: *I don't have a girlfriend like some of the other guys. Should I just stay home?*

A: You don't need a girlfriend to go to a party—or a dance for that matter. In fact, both are great places to meet up with girls, get to know them, and have fun doing it. Go for it!

Q: *I don't know how to dance. I don't want everyone staring at me.*

A: Honestly, most guys don't know how to dance very well. You're probably better than you think, so try not to be too self-conscious. If you feel totally clueless on the dance floor, just watch other people and imitate them. Relax and have a good time.

Q: *Some of the guys have been talking about a kissing game. What if I don't want to play?*

A: Handle it like you would anything you don't want to do. Say, "No thanks" or "Not interested" and walk away.

Q: *What if my old girlfriend from school is there with her new boyfriend?*

A: There's certainly no need to hide out. Remember, you're there to enjoy yourself. If that means you say hello and go your own way, that's okay. If it means you hang out and talk with them the whole evening, that's okay, too. The idea is to get out and have fun. How you do that is your decision.

Q: *My parents won't let me go. What should I do?*

A: Make sure you're being honest with them about the party, who will be there, and who you're going with. Ask your parents to call the parents of the person having the party. There's a chance that if they know more about the party and what sort of adult supervision there will be, they might change their minds and let you go.

Q: *It's a formal and everyone's wearing a tie. Do I have to do the same?*

A: As a general rule, it's best to dress like everyone else. For example, you probably don't want to wear cutoffs and a t-shirt when the other guys are wearing coats and ties. If you want to draw attention to yourself, that's not the way to do it. Just ask around if you're not sure what to wear.

THE SCOOP FROM SOUP:

Some guys don't have a formal suit and tie until they get a little older. If you find yourself in that situation, just wear your nicest shirt and pants. A dress shirt and tie with dress pants looks nice, too. You won't be the only one there without a tie or a suit jacket. The idea is to have fun. Go and enjoy yourself!

Talking To Your Parents

Here's the situation: You've been invited to a party next Saturday at a friend's house. He has a brother who's a high school senior, so there will probably be some older kids there, too. You need your parent's permission to go, but you're a little nervous because you don't know how they'll react. Here are some tips to get off on the right foot when you talk with them:

- Find a time that you and your parents are free to talk without the interruptions of work, cell phones, siblings, and television. Begin by asking them, "Are you free to talk?"

- Get right to the point. "Dad, I need to get your permission to go to a party on Saturday. Can I tell you about it?"

- Give details that will help your parents understand the situation, including where the party is, who will be there, how long it lasts, and when you'll be home.

- No matter how they respond, listen to what they say without interrupting or reacting.

- Try to understand your parents' point of view. If you disagree with them, can you see their side of it? If you can, say so. Telling them you understand their views and feelings will make them more willing to see yours.

- Keep a cool head if things start to heat up. Your parents will think of you as more grown up and capable of making important decisions when they see you behaving maturely.

- Always use a friendly tone of voice. Being respectful makes it much more likely your parents will listen to you and seriously consider your request.

- If your parents say no, it's okay to let them know you're frustrated and upset, but respect their decision. They love you and want to keep you safe.

THE SCOOP FROM SOUP:

Always tell the truth. Don't shade the facts about whether there will be alcohol at the party, for example. Honesty builds trust. Life is good when your parents trust you.

Teasing

Guys tease girls. Girls tease guys. The older you get, the more you'll notice that guys—and girls—use teasing to show they like someone.

The trouble comes when the teasing gets cruel. Some kids—especially guys—don't know where to stop. They tell sexual jokes and make off-color comments about bodies to shock and embarrass others. What they say crosses the boundary of what's considered private and polite. It's a way to draw attention to themselves.

As an example, guys will talk and comment about a girl's body in front of her or within earshot. Or they will joke about something sexual, like kissing or, well, you know...

They want to make the girl blush and laugh. They think their bold talk impresses girls. In reality, it has just the opposite effect.

Sometimes the girl is strong enough to ask the guy to stop. Sometimes she isn't, and the teasing escalates, getting brasher and more sexually oriented. Learn to recognize when things are getting out of control. If you ever find yourself part of any situation like this, put a stop to it on your own. By the time a girl has to ask you to stop, the teasing has already gone way too far.

In the worst cases, guys use teasing and sexually laced talk to humiliate and bully a girl. They may talk about how large or small her breasts are. Guys, or a group of guys, may corner a girl and make sexual remarks for no other reason than to harass and upset her. They may even touch her or themselves in a sexual way without her permission. This is about as bad as it gets.

Here's the deal. Acting this way is wrong. Period. And it can get you in big trouble with parents and teachers—even the police. Look in the mirror and reflect on the way you treat girls. If you need to change, do it now.

THE SCOOP FROM SOUP:

These days, teasing, and its close cousin, harassment, don't just happen in person. The Internet, with its social networks and chat rooms, is filled with abusive talk and innuendo. It's an easy place to get yourself in trouble, so think twice before you post hateful words or an explicit photo. When you hit the Send button, it's too late to take back something you shouldn't have done in the first place, not to mention the damage you've done to another person.

May the Best Man Win

Who runs fastest, throws farthest, jumps highest? Most guys are really competitive when it comes to sports. And what if they're trying to win over a girl? Well, the competition can be fierce when it comes to romance, too.

Here are some common situations you may run into, and how to handle them:

SITUATION #1: You wonder what it would be like to go out with your best friend's steady girlfriend.

HOW TO HANDLE IT: No matter how experienced or inexperienced you are, there's not always a clear line between being friends with a girl and having romantic feelings for her.

Even so, you need to know that this particular girl is off-limits. Try hard to make sure nothing you do or say sends any other message. Aside from the fact that her boyfriend is your best buddy, she's dating someone and it's just not the right thing to do. Back off and leave her alone.

SITUATION #2: You and your best friend both like the same girl.

HOW TO HANDLE IT: This is a tough situation that requires you both to show some maturity—if your friendship is to survive, that is. Start by admitting you both have romantic feelings for her. Lots of times, important details that affect friendships go unsaid between guys. Don't let that happen to you.

In a way, it's kind of funny but not too surprising, that you both like her. You guys hang out all the time, think alike, and have the same tastes, so why wouldn't you like the same girl? Have a few laughs about it. Let the situation play out. She may choose to go out with you, your friend or neither of you. No matter what happens, the main idea is to keep a cool head and remember that he's your best friend.

SITUATION #3: You really like your best friend's girlfriend and she likes you. They haven't been getting along and, truth be told, you're kind of hoping they break up.

HOW TO HANDLE IT: Give them some space to work out their problems. Stepping in before they break up will betray your friend's trust in you and wreck the friendship. If and when they do split up—and after she's had time to get over him—you can go after her with a clear conscience. No matter the timing, though, keep in mind it may still affect you and your buddy's friendship.

SITUATION #4: There's a guy in your science class who won't stop flirting with your girlfriend. It's clear he's trying to steal her away from you.

HOW TO HANDLE IT: Before confronting him, step back and look at how your girlfriend acts when he's around. If she discourages his advances by ignoring him or telling him, "I have a boyfriend," then you don't have to worry. Let her know you appreciate how she handled the situation and be supportive. After all, she can't help it if he finds her attractive.

On the other hand, if she's flirting and leading the guy on, then you need to re-evaluate your relationship. You have three options to choose from:

1. *Live with it.* If you're like most guys, you won't put up with her flirting for long, especially if it's clear she's looking around for a new boyfriend. You have to be able to trust each other for a relationship to work.

2. *Change it.* You can ask her to change. Fact is, though, people don't change unless *they* want to. So it's not likely to happen if her flirting means she's ready to date someone new.

3. *Leave.* The last option is to go your own way and not look back. Walking away sounds easy and simple, but feelings of jealousy and betrayal can make it awfully hard. Remember, though, there are lots of girls out there and this one wasn't the right one for you. Hang in there and be on the lookout. The right girl will come along.

THE SCOOP FROM SOUP:

If a girl runs around on her boyfriend with you, it's a good bet she'll do it again—except next time it'll be you she's running around on.

Girl "Friend"

You and a girl in your neighborhood have been friends for as long as you can remember. You hang out, have fun together—you do what friends do. Recently, your guy friends have started calling her your girlfriend. They ask, "Are you in love?" and, "Is she a good kisser?" Their teasing doesn't bother you that much, but wow, things have sure changed from when you were younger.

GIRLS as Friends *Fact #1*

Having a girl as a friend is a good thing. It gives you the chance to experience the female psyche—the way girls think—without all the emotions and responsibilities that come with a romantic relationship. You'll see girls as regular people, not as items of desire to be put on a pedestal. It can also mean you'll have more realistic expectations about girls when you do get into a romantic relationship.

So what about your friends? Tell them and anyone else who gives you a hard time, "No, we're just friends." Stick to that message, don't react to the teasing and it'll stop before you know it. Don't change a thing when it comes to your girl "friend" and you. After all, she *is* your friend.

GIRLS as Friends *Fact #2*

Friendships with girls occasionally turn romantic. You know she's available, you already know her, and you like hanging out together. Why not take the next step? Pairing up with a girl friend sometimes works out great. Remember that friendship is the foundation of every good romantic relationship.

GIRLS as Friends *Fact #3*

At some point, one or both of you may decide you like being "just friends" better than being boyfriend-girlfriend. It may be easy to go back to the way things were. Then again, it may not be so easy.

If you're thinking about getting romantic with a girl friend, talk it over with her first. Make sure she understands that you value your friendship and want to keep it going no matter what happens. Make a deal about how you'll treat each other if things don't work out. Then stick to it.

Girls and Social Media

You love being on your cell phone
and computer. Who doesn't? With
emails, chat rooms, instant messages,
text messages, and so many social
networks, it's hard to choose among
them. It's how your friends and you
talk, share and meet new people.
How big is your circle of "friends"?
You don't want to be left out, right?

That's okay, but remember there's
another side to social media. No
matter whether you're texting,
chatting or posting your latest
photos, it's the same as being out
in public, face-to-face. Information
about you can be seen by anyone
with a computer or cell phone,
including parents, teachers—and
strangers, some of whom may not

be who they seem to be. It's so easy
and natural to share it all, to feel
safe. Your name, where you live,
how old you are, where you go to
school, what you're thinking, even
your innermost feelings, are there
for everyone to see—*if* you put them
there.

Here are some do's and don'ts:

- Pick a social networking site
  that allows you to control
  what information is public.

- Restrict access to your page to
  a select group of people, such as
  friends from school and your
  family.

- Keep your personal profile
  private. Don't post information
  that can be used to identify you
  or locate you, such as your full
  name, where you go to school,
  address or phone number.
  And don't post other people's
  information, either.

- Post only information you're comfortable with others seeing— and knowing—about you. Once information is posted online, you can't take it back.

- Don't get angry and respond to hateful or hostile emails, chat comments, text messages, or any other messages. You can't win online arguments, so bite your lip—in this case, sit on your hands—and move on.

- Don't befriend strangers you meet in chat rooms or other places; and certainly don't get together with someone you "meet" online. People lie about who they really are. The person you think is a 16-year-old girl may actually be a 35-year-old man.

- Work with your parents when it comes to your phone and computer activities, including when and how long you use them. It doesn't mean you have to give up your privacy, just that you come to an agreement based on mutual trust and understanding.

- If things go bad, get your parents, school counselor or another trusted adult involved right away. It's the responsible thing to do and will help you avoid trouble and embarrassment down the road.

Going Steady

You and your friends have started hanging out with a particular group of girls. You eat together everyday in the lunchroom and meet up whenever you can, for a varsity basketball game or to just hang out and talk on the weekend.

Some of the guys and girls are starting to pair off. Others are just having a good time being part of the group. Either way, you like how it feels to be with a bunch of girls. You still love hanging with just the guys, but the girls make you feel good in a different sort of way.

Just last week, your best friend and one of the girls decided to go steady. It made you think, "Should I do that, too?" Your friend says it's no big deal to date one girl exclusively, but you're not so sure.

It's alright to give it some thought. See what other people, such as your parents, have to say. And listen to what your gut tells you. You have to make sure that if you're going to have a steady girlfriend, it's for the right reason.

And what are the right reasons to go out with just one girl? Let's take a look. Circle the best reasons as you go.

1. Everyone else is doing it.

2. She's a football cheerleader.

3. You feel really great when you're around her.

4. Your best friend says you should.

5. She's the only girl who said yes.

6. You want to make another girl jealous.

7. She's smart, nice and fun to hang out with.

8. It's what guys your age do.

9. You don't want to be left out of the dating scene.

10. She's the best girl you can get.

THE ANSWERS:

Good reasons: 3 and 7

Bad reasons: all the rest

What to Do When You Go Out

There are lots of ways to "go out" with girls. To start, probably the best way is with a group of girls and guys. Groups are good because they take some of the pressure off and give everyone a chance to get comfortable with each other.

It won't be long, though, before you want to go out with just one special girl. When that time comes, there are lots of things you and your girlfriend can do to have fun.

1. Go ice skating.

2. Play miniature golf.

3. Get a bunch of friends together and go bowling.

4. Go for a hike or a walk around your neighborhood.

5. Invite her to meet you at the rec center to go swimming.

6. Attend a school sporting event together.

7. Ask her to the beach with your family for the day.

8. Grab a buddy and meet her and her friends at the pool.

9. Get a pizza together after school.

10. Sit on a park bench and talk.

THE SCOOP FROM SOUP:

It's not so much *where* you are or *what* you're doing, but *who* you're with. What matters most is that you like being around each other.

What NOT to Do When You Go Out

We asked around to find out what bothers girls the most. Here are the top 10 complaints:

1. Talking about previous girlfriends.

2. Texting friends during dinner.

3. Using swear words.

4. Telling lies.

5. Trying too hard to make an impression.

6. Taking phone calls in the middle of a conversation.

7. Ignoring her when you're with a group of people.

8. Showing off.

9. Staring at other girls.

10. Playing mind games.

Okay, let's not focus too much on the bad stuff. We can all make mistakes, especially when we're new at the whole dating game. So, here are the things girls said they liked most:

- Opening the door for her.

- Complimenting her on how she looks.

- Listening to what she has to say.

- Being nice to her friends.

- Treating her with respect.

- Treating her as an equal.

- Doing activities she enjoys and including her in yours.

- Introducing her to your friends and parents.

- Giving her some space while still paying attention to her.

- Being yourself when you're alone with her and when you're around others.

THE SCOOP FROM SOUP:

Showing a girl respect, treating her as an equal, and being yourself are important. If you find yourself doing things from the "what not to do" list, it usually means you're nervous and a little uncomfortable.

Relax and keep in mind that girls like you for who you are, not who you pretend to be. So be yourself and be respectful. Girls like guys who are at ease and self-assured.

Getting Close

To hear other guys talk, everyone but you has been with a girl. Well, don't believe it. Guys like to talk—boast is more like it—especially about their experience with girls. Don't let what other guys have or haven't done affect you. Fact is, the guys who brag most are usually the least experienced. Talking is one thing; doing is another. Don't let all the talk pressure you into doing something you're not ready for.

Kissing and other touching between a girl and a guy happens when the timing is right. Just because your best friend kissed a girl last week doesn't mean you have to rush out and do the same this week. Romance is not a race. Affection between a girl and a guy is most exciting and fun when you know and like each other. Take your time and don't rush things.

With that in mind, here are a few do's and don'ts to guide you:

- Kiss someone because you like her and she likes you.

- Don't force yourself on a girl. If she wants to kiss you, you'll know by how she acts and what she says.

- Make it private. With the exception of weddings, public shows of affection should generally be limited to quick kisses, hugs and handholding. A kiss is for two people, not a crowd. Show respect for yourselves and others around you. Be discreet.

- Don't play the sympathy card to get a kiss. "It's been so long since anyone kissed me," sounds kind of pathetic. It's not a good foundation on which to build a relationship.

- Don't play the guilt card to get a kiss. "If you like me, you'll kiss me," is manipulative, hurtful, and sounds pitiful. Definitely avoid this approach.

- Get out there and meet girls. You'll know when the time is right for the first kiss.

- Oh, and don't be too concerned about the mechanics of kissing. It's more important to be relaxed and have fun. Remember, practice makes perfect!

THE SCOOP FROM SOUP:

At some point, you and your girlfriend may consider taking your physical relationship to the next level. It's a big decision you both should give lots of thought to, regardless of what others brag about and encourage you to do.

The consequences of your decision are huge and can affect the rest of your life. So take some time and think it through. And don't be shy about getting advice from an adult you trust. They've been through this before and can really help you out with the decision.

Is Your Girlfriend the Problem? Or Is It You?

Does she say one thing and do another?

If your girlfriend says, "I'll get us tickets to the movie," do you have a feeling she isn't going to get them because she hardly ever does what she says? Is it because she's forgetful? Too busy? If she honestly means well and tries her best—and you find her forgetfulness an endearing quality— then maybe you can live with it.

Or is she insincere? Do you believe she never intended to get the tickets, or meet you after band practice, or any of the other things she said she'd do and then didn't? If so, you don't trust her because you feel she's being dishonest. By not telling the truth, she isn't giving you the respect you deserve.

Is she neglectful?

Does your girlfriend forget you're there every time the two of you are in a group of people? Before getting too upset, make sure you're not being overly possessive. How much public attention you want from your girlfriend—and she wants from you— depends on a lot of things, including where you are, how long you've known each other, and personal preferences. It's uncommon for two people to have the same expectations all the time. You have to talk about it and agree on what's okay and what's not.

On the other hand, if your girlfriend blatantly flirts with other guys, trying hard to be noticed, demanding their attention, all the while ignoring you, it's time to have a talk. It's good if you hear

her say something like, "I'm sorry.
I didn't mean to make you feel
uncomfortable. I'll stop." But if she
says she'll stop and doesn't, or she
argues with you and says it's your
problem, that's not so good. You
deserve to be treated well. Don't
settle for anything less.

Is she always talking about what's wrong with you?

Does your girlfriend complain a
lot about your relationship with
her? Before deciding, step back and
take another look. Is she generally
supportive of you and do you mostly
have fun being together? Is it possible
things might improve if you took
your girlfriend's advice and made a
few small changes? If so, maybe her
ideas aren't so bad after all.

Then again, does she criticize you
about everything from the way you
look to how you act? Does what
your girlfriend says and how she says
it insult you and make you feel bad?

If it does—and if you see her treat other people the same way—that's not so good. Some people complain and dish out criticism to boost their egos by hurting others. You deserve better than that.

THE SCOOP FROM SOUP:

Accept people—especially girlfriends—for who they are. Don't fool yourself into thinking you can change someone's personality or behavior. Also, don't count on anyone changing for you. Building a relationship on the hope that she'll change is like constructing a skyscraper on a faulty foundation. Sooner or later, they both will fail.

What Bothers Me Most

There are endless ways that guys and girls annoy each other. Here's what some kids had to say about what bothered them when it comes to the opposite sex.

WHAT GIRLS SAY ABOUT BOYS:

THEY don't ever tell you the whole story. —Grace, age 14

BOYS argue and fight about the silliest stuff. —Sydney, age 13

THEY don't consider my feelings. —Allison, age 12

BOYS never show any emotions. And they talk about themselves all the time. —Sarah, age 15

SOME boys pressure girls to do stuff they don't want to. —Hailey, age 15

THEY ignore me when they're with their friends. —Nevaeh, age 13

I HATE when guys think that in order to have fun, they have to spend a lot of money. —Maddie, age 17

YOU can't always take guys seriously. —Laura, age 15

WHEN it's just the two of us, my boyfriend acts differently than when we're with his friends. —Mary, age 15

GUYS don't listen. —Caroline, age 12

WHAT BOYS SAY ABOUT GIRLS:

SHE'S always asking why I don't call her. —Ian, age 14

GIRLS are too possessive when it comes to relationships. They are selfish most of the time. —Diego, age 12

I HATE it when they flirt with other guys. —Wyatt, age 15

THEY can't make up their minds. — Kyle, age 11

THEY change their minds faster than the blink of an eye. —Eli, age 12

THEY'RE too worried about how they look. —Jack, age 13

THEY have these random mood swings I can't explain. —Kevin, age 15

THEY take too long to get ready. — Zack, age 16

GIRLS don't know how to joke around. They take everything I say so literally. —Ryan, age 18

WHEN girls ask for your honest opinion, don't give it. You'll just get in trouble. —Nick, age 17

THE SCOOP FROM SOUP:

The better you know a person the easier it is for them to get under your skin. It happens between family members, between friends, and especially between boyfriends and girlfriends. Because conflict is a part of most relationships, be on the lookout for signs of trouble and learn how to deal with what's bothering you.

Dealing with Problems

You've never been so ticked. You have strong feelings like you've never had before. For that matter, you've never seen your girlfriend so upset, either. Is your relationship over? Should you say, "Just forget it?" Not necessarily.

FIGURE OUT WHAT'S REALLY BOTHERING YOU. Are you sure it's what she said yesterday that's upsetting you? Or is it how she acted at the party Friday night? Are you misunderstanding something and reacting the wrong way? Think it through before you say anything. Figure out why you're upset. You can't fix a problem until you know what it is.

CHOOSE THE RIGHT TIME. Discussions are two-way streets. Make sure enough time has passed to be chilled out. So now, you're ready to talk, but is she? The only way to know is to ask. And whatever you do, don't start the conversation five minutes before you have to catch the bus home. Make sure there's plenty of time, and do it in a private place where you both can talk openly and honestly.

COMMUNICATE. Discussions involve talking and, more importantly, listening. Tell her what you're unhappy about. Next, listen to what she says. Focus on the problem, not the person. You're upset at what happened, not at her. Get the facts out and say what's bothering you. Don't jump to conclusions. Be sure to use "I" when saying what's bugging you. Avoid saying things like, "You made me feel bad." Instead, say, "I was angry over what you said," or, "I don't like it when that happens."

BE PREPARED. No matter how hard you try to stay calm and collected, tempers can flare. She may cry; you may cry, too. Take a break and try again later if things get heated. Nothing ever gets solved by arguing. It's tough, but you need to be able to say, "I'm getting upset again and need to stop talking for now." Let her know you want to work things out, but you need a break.

WORK TOWARD A RESOLUTION. Make sure you let her know what you think has to happen to make the problem go away. Then, once you hear her side of the story, take a look at the options. You can always find middle ground by compromising. But that's not always an option, especially if the problem involves basic values, such as honesty. No matter what the issue, if you just can't come to an agreement, you can always agree to disagree.

MAKE A PLAN. Try to leave the discussion with a plan to make things better. It's not a complete solution, but sometimes just a promise to "call me later" is enough. It's a first step to getting your relationship back on track.

THE SCOOP FROM SOUP:

Be honest with each other. Sometimes relationships can't be fixed. "Making things better" doesn't always mean you stay together. Sometimes it means going your separate ways, and that's okay. Relationships at this age are trial and error. Remaining "just friends" isn't a failure, just part of the learning experience.

Is It Time to Break Up?

It's hard to know exactly when to hang in there and when to call it quits. See how savvy you are when it comes to making a decision. Circle your answers as you go.

SITUATION #1: Your girlfriend is a great person and you've known her a long time, but there's someone else you're starting to like. You don't want to hurt your girlfriend's feelings.

HANG IN THERE or CALL IT QUITS

SITUATION #2: Every time you and your girlfriend plan to meet somewhere, she's late. She always

has a good reason and says she's
sorry, but it's driving you crazy.

HANG IN THERE Or CALL IT QUITS

SITUATION #3: You can't reach your
girlfriend on her cell phone. This has
been going on for a while. When you
ask where she's been, she won't tell
you.

HANG IN THERE Or CALL IT QUITS

SITUATION #4: You guys have been a
couple since 7th grade, but she's been
hard to talk to this week.

HANG IN THERE Or CALL IT QUITS

SITUATION #5: You started going
out with her because she acts and
dresses differently than other girls
you know. Now you realize you
don't have much in common with her
and the differences are beginning to
bother you.

HANG IN THERE Or CALL IT QUITS

THE ANSWERS:

THE best answer to 2 and 4 is HANG IN THERE. Don't throw away a good relationship because of a small or temporary problem. Fix the problem instead.

THE best answer to 1, 3 and 5 is CALL IT QUITS. There's no reason to stick with a girl who treats you badly. Period. And there's no reason to stick with a girl you don't have feelings for. Calling it quits isn't easy. But the hurt will end and you both will get on with finding the right person. Be honest with her—and yourself.

How to Break Up

Nothing stirs up emotions more than ending a relationship. Being on your own again can make you feel lonely and even a little frightened about the future. Or you may feel relieved the relationship is over. After all, it wasn't going well. Or you may feel a little guilty if you ended the relationship for another girl, especially if you said things that now you realize you didn't mean. No matter the reason, though, you need to let her know it's over.

One way is to stop talking to her. You can also tell her everything's okay and act like it's not. Or you can let her figure out the relationship is over on her own. There are lots of nice guys who do cruel things like

these to girls because they don't
know how to handle the situation.

Here's the number one way to break
the news. It's not the easiest, but it's
by far the best.

TELL her face-to-face. Be honest,
but kind. No notes or emails. She
and everyone else will see that as
tactless and maybe even cruel.

KEEP the discussion private.
Announcing your decision
at school or at a party may be
convenient, but it's insensitive and
unnecessary.

PLAN what you're going to say.
Saying, "I think we'd both be
happier if we didn't date any more"
is better than, "You really get on my
nerves." And saying, "I liked it a lot
better when we were just friends"
is better than, "Going out with you
was a big mistake."

DON'T let her hear it from friends.
The relationship was between
you and her. Why should breaking up

be any different? Keep everyone else out of it for now. They'll all know soon enough.

WILL she still be your friend afterwards? It's hard to say. You can be certain the news won't make her smile. More likely, she'll be hurt and maybe even angry—but not nearly as much as if you aren't upfront with her. On the other hand, she may be relieved it's over. No matter what the outcome, though, when all's said and done, it's about being treated fairly.

THE SCOOP FROM SOUP:

Never start running around with another girl before you tell your current girlfriend it's over. Always be honest and strong enough to end one relationship before starting another.

Getting Dumped

Sometimes you know things just
aren't right between you and your
girlfriend. But before you can say
anything, she does. Bam! You've
been dumped. Even though you also
wanted it to end, your ego is pretty
bruised. With a little time, though,
the sting goes away and you're
relieved the relationship's over.

Or maybe you think everything is
going great. Your girlfriend doesn't
show any sign—that you see—of
what she's thinking. Then, one
evening she says she wants to talk.
Bam! You've been dumped. You think,
"Wow, I didn't see that coming." You
feel beat up and upset about what's
happened. A few days pass, and then

a few weeks go by. The feelings don't seem to be going away.

Being dumped is an emotional time, especially if you didn't see it coming. How do you deal with being dumped? First things first, no matter how strong the urge is to hang on and try to change her mind, don't. And whatever you do, don't try to get even. Revenge isn't worth the time and effort.

What happens next? What if the feelings of anger and betrayal won't go away? Deal with it the same way you've learned to deal with other disappointments in your life. Talk it out with a friend or trusted adult. Stay busy physically and mentally. Take what lessons you can from the experience. Keep moving forward. Don't look back.

Just so you'll know, here are the five stages of grief (also known as the Kübler-Ross model) that almost everyone goes through when they experience a loss such as the break-up of a serious relationship. You may find yourself flipping from one emotion to another, and not necessarily in this order. It's the way your mind is programmed to deal with loss. Everyone experiences these emotions at one time or another in their lives. You're not alone.

DENIAL – "This can't be happening to me." This first stage is a temporary defense meant to protect you from the shock of what's happened. It's usually replaced by thoughts of how life is going to be different now that she's gone.

ANGER – "It isn't fair." During the second stage, you're angry and you blame her for what's happened. You might be resentful, jealous or envious of other couples or guys with girlfriends, especially if one of them is with your ex-girlfriend.

BARGAINING – "I'll do anything to get her back." The third stage is based on the hope that things can return to how they were, that there is something you can do to get control over what's happened.

DEPRESSION – "I can't go on without her." It's during the fourth stage that you come to accept that the relationship is over. It's a time when you may feel sad and want to be alone.

ACCEPTANCE – "I'm going to be okay." During the fifth stage you begin coming to terms with the break-up. You realize that life goes on. In time, you begin to look at other girls and think maybe it wouldn't be so bad to try again.

THE SCOOP FROM SOUP:

Take time to heal and feel good about yourself. There's no set amount of time that it takes to feel better. But if it takes longer than a week or two, turn to an adult you trust for support. Before long, you'll be feeling better and ready for the next relationship.

How's It Going?

Take this quiz to find out how the whole girl-guy thing is going for you. Circle your answers.

QUESTION #1: You're absolutely, positively *in love* with your girlfriend and don't want to be with anyone but her.

ME or NOT ME

QUESTION #2: You can't get a date. You figure there must be something wrong with you.

ME or NOT ME

QUESTION #3: Your girlfriend asked you to go with her

to a party this weekend. She knows
you and your Dad are scheduled
to leave Friday for a camping trip,
but she wants you to go with her
anyway. You say okay, because she's
more important than anything else in
your life.

ME Or NOT ME

QUESTION #4: The only
girls interested in you are the ones
no one else wants to go out with.
You don't think you're handsome
enough to go out with a pretty girl.

ME Or NOT ME

QUESTION #5: You were
out with your friends and ran into
the new girl from school. She flirted
with you and asked you to a dance
in her old neighborhood. You figured
your girlfriend wouldn't find out so
you said okay.

ME Or NOT ME

THE ANSWERS:

Read on if you answered ME to any of the questions.

QUESTION #1: LOOK

around. You can probably count on one hand the number of steady couples who've been together more than a month. The point is that girlfriends will come and go in your life.

Good friends—guys and girls—will always be there for you. Don't be a guy who gets a girlfriend and his friends never hear from him again— until they break up, that is. Find time for your new girlfriend and your old friends.

QUESTION #2: First off,

there's nothing wrong with you. Don't judge yourself by the number of girls who are interested in you. Fact is, some guys don't date until after high school.

It's more important that you be yourself—a nice guy with character. So be patient, the right girl for you is out there. If they haven't yet, girls will notice you soon enough. Guaranteed.

QUESTION #3: Think

about it. It's not fair for your girlfriend to demand that you give up the camping trip with your Dad so you can attend a party with her. If something really important and unexpected had come up, like a funeral, that would be different. But a last-minute party? The camping trip was planned weeks ago, and she's known about it from the beginning.

It's hard to keep your self-respect when you allow yourself to be manipulated. Instead, share with her what this trip means to you. Let her know you want to be with her, but the trip is important, too. When all is said and done, your girlfriend will respect you more for being true to yourself than for going to the party with her.

QUESTION #4: First

things first. You're being too hard on yourself. Who's handsome and who's not depends on who's doing the looking. Different looks appeal to different girls. Think about how boring it would be if we all looked the same.

How you act and feel inside is what makes you appealing to girls. Don't buy in to the Hollywood movie version of who's handsome and who's not. Or, for that matter, which girl is pretty and which is not.

QUESTION #5: Trust is

what makes relationships work. And to have trust, you have to be honest. If you've been thinking about breaking up with your girlfriend, this isn't the way to do it. Be honest with her first, and then go out with the new girl. If you plan on staying with your girlfriend and you're going out with the new girl just for fun, you need to grow up. It sounds like you're not ready to have a steady girlfriend.

Just Around the Corner

You're older now. You know more about the girl-guy thing than you did previously. You've had your first crush and survived it. You go to dances and parties and hang out with groups of guys and girls. You feel more comfortable around girls than you used to. And you're starting to wonder what it would be like to have a steady girlfriend.

Relationships are complicated, and there are lots of ups and downs. They work best when both people feel good about themselves. Sure, a steady girlfriend would be great, but your happiness doesn't, and shouldn't, depend on having one. While you're looking around, spend time getting to know *you*. It will make you strong

and confident and ready for the girl
of your dreams when she comes
along.

You're off to a great start! There are
new people, new adventures, and
tons of great new things waiting
for you just around the corner.
Remember, relationships are a
learning process—at times maybe
a bit scary—but a fun experience
nonetheless. You're on your way.
Now go out and experience it all!

The Authors

GARY J. CAMPBELL is a licensed school counselor and social worker with over 23 years hands-on experience. "Soup," as the students at Meyer Middle School affectionately call him, holds a Guidance & Counseling M.S. and B.S.W. degree. Gary, an outspoken advocate for programs and services that create success for children and families, is on the Board of the Wisconsin School Counselor Association, a member of the St. Croix Valley Restorative Justice Board and is faculty representative for the school district's educational foundation. When he's not writing books or helping the community, Gary divides his remaining time between 650+

students, his wife, Dawn, and their three children, Mackenzie, Olivia, and Ethan.

*F*RANK C. HAWKINS, father of two teenagers, writes books that make young men and women think, sweat and laugh—though not necessarily in that order. He is author of the *Boy's Body Guide, Boy's Fitness Guide, Girl's Fitness Guide,* and *Book of Bad Habits for Young (and Not So Young!) Men and Women.*